The
British
Pub
Cookbook

The British Pub Cookbook

TRADITIONAL AND
CONTEMPORARY
RECIPES FOR PERFECT
PUB FOOD

First published in 2011
LOVE FOOD is an imprint of Parragon Books Ltd

Parragon
Queen Street House
4 Queen Street
Bath BA1 1HE, UK

www.parragon.com

ISBN: 978-1-4454-4451-2

Printed in China

Notes for the Reader
This book uses both metric and imperial measurements. Follow the same units of measurement throughout; do not mix metric and imperial. All spoon measurements are level: teaspoons are assumed to be 5 ml, and tablespoons are assumed to be 15 ml. Unless otherwise stated, milk is assumed to be full fat, eggs and individual vegetables are medium, and pepper is freshly ground black pepper.

The times given are an approximate guide only. Preparation times differ according to the techniques used by different people and the cooking times may also vary from those given. Optional ingredients, variations or serving suggestions have not been included in the calculations.

Recipes using raw or very lightly cooked eggs should be avoided by infants, the elderly, pregnant women, convalescents and anyone suffering from an illness. Pregnant and breastfeeding women are advised to avoid eating peanuts and peanut products. Sufferers from nut allergies should be aware that some of the ready-made ingredients used in the recipes in this book may contain nuts. Always check the packaging before use.

The publisher would like to thank the following for permission to reproduce copyright material:

Front cover images –The Boot pub, Sarrat © Robin Bush/Getty Images and Chalk white horse © Peter Denton/Getty Images
Internal images – Pg 7 Stonehenge © Grant Faint/Getty Images, pg 9 The Mussenden temple © Neale Clarke/Getty Images, pg 31 The Boot pub, Sarrat © Robin Bush/Getty Images, pg 44 Dunluce Castle © Brian Lawrence/Getty Images, pg 55 White Cliffs Of Dover © Don Klumpp/ Getty Images, pg 86 Two people standing on the Giant's Causeway in County Antrim © Getty Images
Additional images on pages 22, 24, 37, 70, 73, 78 and 84 courtesy of Istock.

Contents

Introduction   6

Chapter 1 Light Bites   8

Chapter 2 Classic Pub Grub   30

Chapter 3 Weekend Wonders 54

Chapter 4 To Finish   76

Index   96

Introduction

The British pub is a unique institution quite unlike the bars and cafés of the Continent or even the pubs in Australia and New Zealand. But to talk about British pubs as if they are all the same is misleading, especially in light of all the changes that have taken place in the last couple of decades. One of the great things about British pubs is that they are so varied. The smart city pub is the perfect place to meet friends for a quick snack and a glass of wine before setting off for the theatre or cinema, while a family-friendly country pub is ideal for relaxing in the garden during the summer and in front of a roaring fire in the winter and enjoying a delicious and prolonged weekend lunch. Pubs are great places to catch up with friends for a social evening and just as good for winding down before the commute home after a busy day at work.

Traditional pub food has a special place in British culture and the recipes in the following four chapters are all long-established, firm favourites. Light Bites, whether a plate of freshly-made sandwiches, a crisp Cornish pasty or a tasty pie, is the chapter for easy snacks and quick lunches. Classic Pub Grub is packed with recipes for much-loved, more substantial dishes that range from Steak & Kidney Pudding to Sausage & Mash with Onion Gravy. Weekend Wonders offers a tempting array of roasts, as well as scrumptious pies and classic salmon. Last, but by no means least, To Finish celebrates another uniquely British institution – the pudding – featuring hot and cold traditional treats from Treacle Tart and Sticky Toffee Pudding to Eton Mess and Home-made Crackers served with some of Britain's excellent cheese.

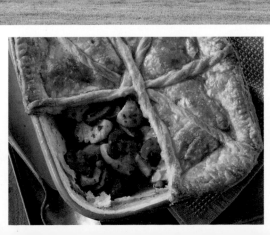

Chapter 1

Light Bites

Broccoli & Stilton Soup

Serves 4

50 g/1¾ oz butter
2 onions, chopped
1 potato, peeled and diced
1 litre/1¾ pints hot vegetable
  stock or chicken stock
1 head broccoli, broken into
  small florets
200 ml/7 fl oz double cream
200 g/7 oz Stilton or other firm
  blue cheese, crumbled
4 slices of French bread, toasted
pepper
10 g/¼ oz snipped fresh chives,
  to garnish

Heat the butter in a large saucepan over a medium heat. Add the onions and cook, stirring frequently, for 5–8 minutes, or until soft. Add the potato and stir, then add the stock and bring to the boil. Reduce the heat and simmer for 5 minutes.

Add the broccoli and cook, stirring occasionally, for a further 5 minutes. Season to taste with pepper. Transfer the soup to a food processor or blender, in batches, and process until smooth. Return to a clean saucepan.

Add 150 ml/5 fl oz of the cream and 150 g/5½ oz of the cheese to the soup and cook over a low heat, stirring, until the cheese has melted.

Mash the remaining cheese with the remaining cream in a bowl and pile some onto each of the toast slices.

Serve the soup hot in individual warmed bowls, topped with the cheesy toast slices and sprinkled with a few chives.

LYME REGIS, ENGLAND

Quiche Lorraine

Serves 4

4 eggs
175 g/6 oz cooked ham
3 spring onions, finely chopped
150 ml/5 fl oz milk, plus extra to
  glaze
salt and pepper

pastry
250 g/9 oz plain flour
115 g/4 oz butter
pinch of salt
2–3 tbsp cold water, to mix

Preheat the oven to 200°C/400°F/Gas Mark 6.

To make the pastry, put the flour into a bowl, rub in the butter until the mixture resembles fine breadcrumbs, then add the salt and enough water to make a smooth dough.

Bring a saucepan of water to the boil. Gently lower 2 of the eggs into the water using a long-handled spoon. Keep the water at a gentle simmer and cook for 8 minutes. Remove the eggs and cool under cold running water.

Divide the pastry in two, one piece slightly larger than the other, and roll out the larger piece to line a 20-cm/8-inch flan tin.

Peel the hard-boiled eggs carefully and wipe to make sure there are no pieces of shell attached to the eggs. Chop the eggs and cut the ham into small pieces. Place the eggs, ham and onions in the pastry case.

Beat the remaining eggs with the milk, season well with salt and pepper and pour over the ham mixture.

Roll out the other piece of pastry, dampen the edge of the pastry base and lay the lid on top. Seal well and crimp the edges of the quiche. Glaze with a little milk and place the quiche on a baking sheet.

Bake in the preheated oven for 10 minutes then reduce the oven temperature to 180°C/350°F/Gas Mark 4 and bake for a further 30 minutes, until the pastry is golden. Serve warm or cold.

Pork & Apple Pie

Serves 8

900 g/2 lb waxy potatoes,
  peeled and sliced
2 tbsp butter
2 tbsp vegetable oil
450 g/1 lb lean boneless pork,
  cubed
2 onions, sliced
4 garlic cloves, crushed
600 ml/1 pint stock
2 tbsp chopped fresh sage
2 eating apples, peeled,
  cored and sliced
1 egg, beaten
1 tsp gelatine
salt and pepper

pastry
675 g/1 lb 8 oz plain flour,
  plus extra for dusting
pinch of salt
4 tbsp butter
125 g/4½ oz lard
300 ml/10 fl oz water

Bring a large saucepan of lightly salted water to the boil, add the potatoes and cook for 10 minutes. Drain and set aside. Melt the butter with the oil in a flameproof casserole dish over a medium–high heat. Add the pork and cook until browned all over.

Add the onions and garlic and cook, stirring frequently, for 5 minutes. Stir in the pork, stock and sage. Season to taste with salt and pepper. Reduce the heat, cover and simmer for 1½ hours. Drain the stock from the casserole dish and reserve. Leave the pork to cool.

Preheat the oven to 200°C/400°F/Gas Mark 6. To make the pastry, sift the flour and salt into a bowl. Make a well in the centre. Melt the butter and lard in a saucepan with the water, then bring to the boil. Pour into the well and gradually mix into the flour to form a dough. Turn out onto a lightly floured surface and knead until smooth.

Reserve a quarter of the dough and use the remainder to line the base and sides of a large pie tin or deep 20-cm/8-inch round loose-based cake tin. Alternatively, use the dough to line eight individual tart tins.

Layer the pork, potatoes and apples in the base of the tin or tins. Roll out the reserved pastry to make a lid. Dampen the edges with water and put the lid on top, sealing well. Brush with the beaten egg to glaze. Make a hole in the top. Bake in the preheated oven for 30 minutes, then reduce the temperature to 160°C/325°F/Gas Mark 3 and bake for a further 45 minutes. Dissolve the gelatine in the reserved stock and pour into the hole in the lid as the pie cools. Serve well chilled.

Classic Sandwich Selection

Serves 8–10

32 slices thinly sliced
 white or brown bread
55 g/2 oz butter, softened
salt and pepper

egg & cress
4 hard-boiled eggs,
 shelled and chopped
2 tbsp mayonnaise
½ punnet fresh cress

cucumber
½ cucumber, finely sliced

roast beef & horseradish
115 g/4 oz sliced rare roast beef
2 tbsp creamed horseradish

smoked salmon & cream cheese
115 g/4 oz cream cheese
4 slices smoked salmon
juice of 1 lemon

Cut off the bread crusts with a serrated knife and butter each slice.

For the Egg & Cress sandwiches mix the egg with the mayonnaise. Cut the cress from the punnet with a pair of scissors and stir into the mixture. Divide the mixture between 4 slices of bread, season to taste and top with another 4 slices of bread. Cut to shape.

For the Cucumber sandwiches arrange the cucumber on 4 slices of bread and season with lots of pepper. Top with another 4 slices of bread and cut to shape.

For the Roast Beef & Horseradish sandwiches arrange the beef on 4 slices of bread and spread another 4 slices with the horseradish sauce. Layer together and cut to shape.

For the Smoked Salmon & Cream Cheese sandwiches spread the cheese on 4 slices of bread (you can omit the butter from these slices) and arrange the smoked salmon on top. Sprinkle with lemon juice and season with pepper. Top with another 4 slices of bread and cut to shape.

Serve immediately.

 # Mustard Steak Sandwiches

Serves 4

8 slices thick white or brown bread
butter, for spreading
2 handfuls mixed salad leaves
3 tbsp olive oil
2 onions, thinly sliced
675 g/1 lb 8 oz rump or sirloin
  steak, about 2.5 cm/1 inch thick
1 tbsp Worcestershire sauce
2 tbsp wholegrain mustard
2 tbsp water
salt and pepper

Spread each slice of bread with some butter and add a few salad leaves to the bottom slices.

Heat 2 tablespoons of the oil in a large, heavy-based frying pan over a medium heat. Add the onions and cook, stirring occasionally, for 10–15 minutes until softened and golden brown. Using a slotted spoon, transfer to a plate and set aside.

Increase the heat to high and add the remaining oil to the pan. Add the steak, season with pepper to taste and cook quickly on both sides to seal. Reduce the heat to medium and cook, turning once, for 2½–3 minutes each side for rare or 3½–5 minutes each side for medium. Transfer the steak to the plate with the onions.

Add the Worcestershire sauce, mustard and water to the pan and stir, scraping any sediment from the base of the pan. Return the onions to the pan, season with salt and pepper to taste and mix well.

Thinly slice the steak across the grain, divide it between the 4 bottom halves of bread and cover with the onions. Cover with the top halves of bread and press down gently. Serve immediately.

Fish Cakes

Serves 4

450 g/1lb floury potatoes, such as King Edward, Maris Piper or Desirée, peeled and cut into chunks
450 g/1lb mixed fish fillets, such as cod and salmon, skinned
2 tbsp chopped fresh tarragon
grated rind of 1 lemon
2 tbsp double cream
1 tbsp plain flour
1 egg, beaten
115 g/4 oz breadcrumbs, made from day-old white or brown bread
salt and pepper
4 tbsp vegetable oil, for frying
watercress salad and lemon wedges, to serve

Bring a large saucepan of lightly salted water to the boil, add the potatoes and cook for 15–20 minutes. Drain well and mash with a potato masher until smooth.

Place the fish in a frying pan and just cover with water. Bring to the boil over a medium heat, then reduce the heat, cover the pan and simmer gently for 5 minutes until cooked.

Remove the pan from the heat and drain the fish onto a plate. When cool enough to handle, flake the fish roughly into good-sized pieces, ensuring that there are no bones.

Mix the potato with the fish, tarragon, lemon rind and cream.Season well with salt and pepper and shape into 4 round cakes or 8 smaller ones.

Dust the cakes with flour and dip them into the beaten egg, then coat thoroughly with the breadcrumbs. Place on a baking tray and leave to chill in the refrigerator for at least 30 minutes.

Heat the oil in the pan, add the cakes and fry over a medium heat for 5 minutes on each side, turning them carefully with a palette knife or a fish slice.

Serve immediately with watercress salad and lemon wedges.

Welsh Rarebit

Serves 4

4 thick slices white or brown bread
225 g/8 oz mature Cheddar cheese, grated
25 g/1 oz butter
3 tbsp beer
½ tsp mustard powder
1 egg, beaten
salt and pepper

Preheat the grill to medium. Toast the bread under the grill on one side only.

Put the cheese into a saucepan and add the butter and beer. Heat slowly over a low heat, stirring continuously. Add some salt and pepper and the mustard powder and stir well until the mixture is thick and creamy. Remove from the heat and leave to cool slightly before mixing in the egg.

Increase the grill heat to high. Spread the rarebit generously over the untoasted side of the bread and place under the grill until golden and bubbling. Serve immediately.

STRUMBLE HEAD LIGHTHOUSE, WALES

Bubble & Squeak

Serves 2–3

450 g/1 lb floury potatoes, such
    as King Edward, Maris Piper or
    Desirée, peeled and cut into
    chunks
55 g/2 oz butter
3 tbsp hot milk
450 g/1 lb green cabbage
4 tbsp olive oil
1 onion, thinly sliced
salt and pepper

Bring a large saucepan of lightly salted water to the boil, add the potatoes and cook for 15–20 minutes. Drain well and mash with a potato masher until smooth. Season with salt and pepper, add the butter and milk and stir well.

Cut the cabbage into quarters, remove the stalk and finely shred the leaves. Put half the oil into a large frying pan, add the onion and fry until soft. Add the cabbage to the pan and stir-fry for 2–3 minutes until soft. Season with salt and pepper, add the potato and mix together well.

Press the mixture firmly into the frying pan and leave to cook over a high heat for 4–5 minutes until the base is crispy. Place a plate over the pan and invert the pan so that the potato cake falls onto the plate. Add the remaining oil to the pan, reheat and slip the cake back into the pan with the uncooked side down.

Continue to cook for a further 5 minutes until the base is crispy. Turn out onto a warmed plate and cut into wedges for serving. Serve immediately.

LAND'S END, ENGLAND

Cornish Pasties

Serves 4

250 g/9 oz chuck steak, trimmed
   and cut into 1-cm/½-inch dice
175 g/6 oz swede, peeled and cut
   into 1-cm/½-inch dice
350 g/12 oz potatoes, peeled and
   cut into 1-cm/½-inch dice
1 onion, finely chopped
1 egg, beaten
butter, for greasing
salt and pepper

pastry
450 g/1 lb plain flour,
   plus extra for dusting
pinch of salt
115 g/4 oz lard
115 g/4 oz butter
175 ml/6 fl oz cold water,
   plus extra for brushing

To make the pastry, sift the flour and salt into a bowl and gently rub in the lard and butter until the mixture resembles breadcrumbs. Add the water, a spoonful at a time, and stir the mixture with a knife until it holds together.

Turn out onto a lightly floured surface and gently press together until smooth. Wrap in clingfilm and leave to chill in the refrigerator for 1 hour.

Meanwhile, to prepare the filling, mix the meat and vegetables together and season well with salt and pepper.

Divide the pastry into 4 even-sized pieces and roll one out until just larger than the size of a 20-cm/8-inch plate. Place the plate on top of the pastry and cut round it to give a neat edge. Repeat with the other pieces.

Arrange the meat and vegetable mixture across the 4 rounds of pastry, making sure the filling goes almost to the edge.

Brush the edges of the pastry with water, then bring the edges up over the filling and press together to form a ridge. You can flute the edges of the pasties with your fingers or fold over the pastry to form a cord-like seal. Tuck in the ends. Leave to chill for 1 hour, then glaze with the egg.

Meanwhile, preheat the oven to 190°C/375°F/Gas Mark 5 and grease a baking tray.

Place the pasties on the baking tray and cook in the centre of the preheated oven for 50–60 minutes. The pasties should be crisp and golden in colour. If the pastry is getting too brown, cover with foil and reduce the oven temperature. Serve warm.

Scotch Eggs

Serves 6

4 large eggs
300 g/10½ oz good-quality
    sausage meat
1 tbsp plain flour, plus extra
    for dusting
1 egg, beaten
100 g/3½ oz fresh breadcrumbs
vegetable oil, for deep-frying
salt and pepper
mixed green salad, to serve

Bring a saucepan of water to the boil. Gently lower the eggs into the water using a long-handled spoon. Keep the water at a gentle simmer and cook for 8 minutes. Remove the eggs and cool under cold running water. Peel carefully and wipe to make sure there are no pieces of shell attached to the eggs.

Divide the sausage meat into 4 equal portions and flatten out into rounds on a floured surface – they should be large enough to enclose the eggs.

Mix the flour with the salt and pepper to taste and put on a plate.

Put the beaten egg in a small bowl and the fresh breadcrumbs into a larger container.

Drop the eggs, one at a time, into the flour and then work the sausage meat around each egg until they are a good shape and have a smooth appearance. Brush with beaten egg and then toss in the breadcrumbs until evenly coated.

Heat enough oil for deep-frying in a large saucepan or deep-fryer to 180–190°C/350–375°F, or until a cube of bread browns in 30 seconds. Fry the eggs for 6–8 minutes until they are golden brown. Remove them from the pan and drain well on kitchen paper. If using a saucepan, only cook 2 of the Scotch eggs at a time to be safe.

Slice the Scotch eggs in half and serve immediately with a green salad.

Chapter 2

Classic Pub Grub

Fish & Chips

Serves 2

vegetable oil, for deep-frying
3 large potatoes, such as Cara
  or Desirée
2 thick cod or haddock fillets,
  175 g/6 oz each
175 g/6 oz self-raising flour,
  plus extra for dusting
200 ml/7 fl oz cold lager
salt and pepper
tartare sauce, to serve

Heat enough oil for deep-frying in a large saucepan or deep-fryer to 120°C/250°F, checking the temperature with a thermometer, to blanch the chips. Preheat the oven to 150°C/300°F/Gas Mark 2.

Peel the potatoes and cut into even-sized chips. Fry for about 8–10 minutes, depending on size, until soft but not coloured. Remove from the oil, drain on kitchen paper and place in a warmed dish in the preheated oven. Increase the temperature of the oil to 180–190°C/350–375°F, or until a cube of bread browns in 30 seconds.

Meanwhile, season the fish with salt and pepper and dust lightly with flour.

Make a thick batter by sifting the flour into a bowl with a little salt and whisking in most of the lager. Check the consistency of the batter before adding the remaining lager: it should be very thick like double cream.

Dip one fillet into the batter and allow the batter to coat it thickly. Carefully place the fish in the hot oil, then repeat with the other fillet.

Cook for 8–10 minutes, depending on the thickness of the fish. Turn over the fillets halfway through the cooking time. Remove the fish from the fryer, drain and keep warm.

Return the chips to the fryer at the increased temperature and cook for a further 2–3 minutes until they are golden brown and crisp. Drain and season with salt and pepper before serving with the battered fish and tartare sauce.

Steak & Kidney Pudding

Serves 4

butter, for greasing
450 g/1 lb braising steak, trimmed
   and cut into 2.5-cm/1-inch pieces
2 lambs' kidneys, cored and cut
   into 2.5-cm/1-inch pieces
55 g/2 oz flour
1 onion, finely chopped
115 g/4 oz large field mushrooms,
   sliced (optional)
1 tbsp chopped fresh parsley
about 300 ml/10 fl oz stock,
   or a mixture of beer and water
salt and pepper

suet pastry
350 g/12 oz self-raising flour
175 g/6 oz suet
225 ml/8 fl oz cold water
salt and pepper

Grease a 1.2-litre/2-pint pudding basin.

Put the prepared meat into a large plastic bag with the flour and salt and pepper to taste and shake well until all the meat is well coated. Add the onion, mushrooms, if using, and the parsley and shake again.

Make the suet pastry by mixing together the flour, suet and salt and pepper to taste. Add enough of the cold water to make a soft dough.

Keep a quarter of the dough to one side and roll the remainder out to form a circle big enough to line the pudding basin. Line the basin, making sure that there is a good 1 cm/½ inch hanging over the edge.

Place the meat mixture in the basin and pour in enough of the stock to cover the meat.

Roll out the remaining pastry to make a lid. Fold in the edges of the pastry, dampen them and place the lid on top. Seal firmly in place.

Cover with a piece of greaseproof paper and then foil, with a pleat to allow for expansion during cooking, and seal well. Place in a steamer or large saucepan half filled with boiling water. Simmer the pudding for 4–5 hours, topping up the water from time to time.

Remove the basin from the steamer and take off the coverings. Wrap a clean cloth around the basin and serve immediately.

Lancashire Hotpot

Serves 4–6

900 g/2 lb best end lamb chops
3 lambs' kidneys, cored
  and quartered
55 g/2 oz butter
900 g/2 lb floury potatoes,
  such as King Edward or Maris
  Piper, peeled and sliced
3 onions, halved
  and finely sliced
2 tsp fresh thyme leaves
1 tsp finely chopped
  fresh rosemary
600 ml/1 pint chicken stock
salt and pepper

Preheat the oven to 160°C/325°F/Gas Mark 3.

Trim the chops of any excess fat and place in a bowl. Add the kidneys to the bowl and season with salt and pepper to taste.

Grease a large, shallow ovenproof dish or deep roasting tin with half the butter and arrange a layer of potatoes in the bottom. Layer up the onions and meat, seasoning with salt and pepper to taste and sprinkling in the herbs between each layer. Finish with a neat layer of overlapping potatoes.

Pour in most of the stock so that it covers the meat.

Melt the remaining butter and brush the top of the potato with it. Reserve any remaining butter. Cover with foil and cook in the preheated oven for 2 hours.

Uncover the hotpot and brush the potatoes again with the melted butter. Return the hotpot to the oven and cook for a further 30 minutes, or until the potatoes are crisp and brown.

Serve immediately.

BURNSALL BRIDGE, ENGLAND

Gammon Steaks with Fried Egg & Chips

Serves 4

vegetable oil, for frying and
  brushing
6 large potatoes, such as Desirée or
  Maris Piper, peeled and cut into
  even-sized chips
4 x 175 g/6 oz gammon steaks
4 eggs

Heat enough oil for deep-frying in a large saucepan or deep-fryer to 120°C/250°F, checking the temperature with a thermometer, to blanch the chips. Preheat the oven to 150°C/300°F/Gas Mark 2.

Fry the chips for about 8–10 minutes, depending on size, until soft but not coloured. Remove from the oil, drain on kitchen paper and place in a warmed dish in the preheated oven. Increase the temperature of the oil to 180-190°C/350-375°F, or until a cube of bread browns in 30 seconds.

Meanwhile, place the gammon steaks on a grill pan and brush with a little oil. Preheat the grill to high and grill for 3-4 minutes on either side, turning occasionally until the fat is crisp. Set aside and keep warm.

Return the chips to the fryer at the increased temperature and cook for a further 2–3 minutes until they are golden brown and crisp. Drain, season well and keep warm.

Put 2 tablespoons of oil into a frying pan and heat over a medium heat. Break two eggs into the pan and cook for a few seconds until the white is setting. Tip the pan and spoon the hot oil over the egg yolks so that they become firm but still soft. Remove the eggs from the pan using a wooden spatula and drain on kitchen paper. Keep warm and repeat with the other eggs.

Arrange the gammon steaks, egg and chips on warmed plates and serve immediately.

Sausage & Mash with Onion Gravy

Serves 4–6

8 good-quality sausages
1 tbsp oil

onion gravy
3 onions, halved and thinly sliced
70 g/2½ oz butter
125 ml/4 fl oz Marsala or port
125 ml/4 fl oz vegetable stock
salt and pepper

mash
900 g/2 lb floury potatoes, such
  as King Edward, Maris Piper or
  Desirée, peeled and cut into
  chunks
55 g/2 oz butter
3 tbsp hot milk
2 tbsp chopped fresh parsley

Put the sausages in a frying pan with the oil and cook slowly over a low heat for 25–30 minutes. Cover the pan and turn the sausages from time to time. Don't rush the cooking, because you want them well-cooked and sticky.

Meanwhile, prepare the onion gravy. Add the onions to a frying pan with the butter and fry over a low heat, stirring constantly, until soft. Continue to cook for about 30 minutes, until the onions are brown and almost melting, stirring from time to time.

Pour in the Marsala and stock and continue to bubble away until the onion gravy is really thick. Season to taste with salt and pepper.

To make the mash, bring a large saucepan of lightly salted water to the boil. Add the potatoes and cook for 15–20 minutes. Drain well and mash with a potato masher until smooth. Season with salt and pepper, add the butter, milk and parsley and stir well.

Serve the sausages really hot with the mash. Spoon a generous serving of the onion gravy over the top.

Beef Stew with Dumplings

Serves 4–6

3 tbsp olive oil
2 onions, finely sliced
2 garlic cloves, chopped
1 kg/2 lb 4 oz good-quality
  braising steak
2 tbsp plain flour
300 ml/10 fl oz beef stock
bouquet garni
150 ml/5 fl oz red wine
salt and pepper
1 tbsp chopped fresh flat-leaf
  parsley, to garnish

dumplings
115 g/4 oz self-raising flour,
  plus extra for shaping
55 g/2 oz suet or vegetable
  shortening
1 tsp mustard
1 tbsp chopped fresh parsley
1 tsp chopped fresh sage
4 tbsp cold water

Preheat the oven to 150°C/300°F/Gas Mark 2.

Heat 1 tablespoon of the oil in a large frying pan, then add the onions and garlic and fry until soft and brown. Remove from the pan using a slotted spoon and place in a large casserole dish.

Trim the meat and cut into thick strips. Add the remaining oil to the pan, then add the meat and fry over a high heat, stirring well, until brown all over.

Sprinkle in the flour and stir well to prevent lumps forming. Season well with salt and pepper.

Reduce the heat to medium, pour in the stock, stirring all the time to make a smooth sauce, then continue to heat until boiling.

Carefully turn the contents of the pan into the casserole dish. Add the bouquet garni and the wine. Cover and cook gently in the preheated oven for 2–2½ hours.

Start making the dumplings 20 minutes before the stew is ready. Place the flour, suet, mustard, parsley, sage and salt and pepper to taste in a bowl and mix well. Add enough of the water to the mixture to form a firm but soft dough. Break the dough into pieces and roll them into round dumplings (you might need some flour on your hands for this).

Remove the stew from the oven, check the seasoning, discard the bouquet garni and add the dumplings, pushing them down under the liquid. Cover and return the dish to the oven for 15 minutes, or until the dumplings have doubled in size.

Serve piping hot with the parsley scattered over the top.

Irish Stew

Serves 4–6

4 tbsp plain flour
1.3 kg/3 lb middle neck of lamb, trimmed of visible fat
3 large onions, chopped
3 carrots, sliced
450 g/1 lb potatoes, quartered
½ tsp dried thyme
850 ml/1½ pints hot beef stock
salt and pepper
2 tbsp chopped fresh flat-leaf parsley, to garnish

Preheat the oven to 160°C/325°F/Gas Mark 3. Spread the flour on a plate and season with salt and pepper. Roll the pieces of lamb in the flour to coat, shaking off any excess, and arrange in the base of a casserole dish.

Layer the onions, carrots and potatoes on top of the lamb.

Sprinkle in the thyme and pour in the stock, then cover and cook in the preheated oven for 2½ hours. Garnish with the parsley and serve straight from the casserole dish.

DUNLUCE CASTLE, NORTHERN IRELAND

Coronation Chicken

Serves 6

4 boneless chicken breasts
1 bay leaf
1 small onion, sliced
1 carrot, sliced
4 peppercorns
1 tbsp olive oil
2 shallots, finely chopped
2 tsp mild curry paste
2 tsp tomato purée
juice of ½ lemon
300 ml/10 fl oz mayonnaise
150 ml/5 fl oz natural yogurt
85 g/3 oz ready-to-eat dried
  apricots, chopped
salt and pepper
2 tbsp chopped fresh flat-leaf
  parsley, to garnish

Place the chicken breasts in a large saucepan with the bay leaf, onion and carrot. Cover with water and add half a teaspoon of salt and the peppercorns. Bring to the boil over a medium heat, reduce the heat and simmer very gently for 20–25 minutes. Remove from the heat and allow to cool in the liquor. Drain off 150 ml/5 fl oz of the stock for the sauce.

Meanwhile, heat the oil in a frying pan, add the shallots and sauté gently for 2–3 minutes until soft but not coloured. Stir in the curry paste and continue to cook for a further minute. Stir in the reserved stock, the tomato purée and the lemon juice and simmer for 10 minutes until the sauce is quite thick. Leave to cool.

Remove the chicken from the stock, take off the skin and slice the meat into neat pieces.

Mix together the mayonnaise and the yogurt and stir into the sauce. Add the chopped apricots and season to taste with salt and pepper.

Stir the chicken into the sauce until well coated and place in a serving dish. Leave to stand for at least 1 hour to allow the flavours to mingle. Serve garnished with the parsley.

Fisherman's Pie

Serves 4–6

900 g/2 lb white fish fillets,
  such as plaice, skinned
150 ml/5 fl oz dry white wine
1 tbsp chopped fresh parsley,
  tarragon or dill
175 g/6 oz small mushrooms,
  sliced
100 g/3½ oz butter, plus extra
  for greasing
175 g/6 oz cooked, peeled prawns
40 g/1½ oz plain flour
125 ml/4 fl oz double cream
900 g/2 lb floury potatoes, such
  as King Edward, Maris Piper or
  Desirée, peeled and cut into
  chunks
salt and pepper

Preheat the oven to 180°C/350°F/Gas Mark 4. Grease a 1.7-litre/3-pint baking dish.

Fold the fish fillets in half and place in the dish. Season well with salt and pepper, pour over the wine and scatter over the herbs. Cover with foil and bake for 15 minutes until the fish starts to flake. Strain off the liquid and reserve for the sauce. Increase the oven temperature to 220°C/425°F/Gas Mark 7.

Add the mushrooms to a frying pan with 15 g/½ oz of the butter and sauté. Spoon the mushrooms over the fish and scatter over the prawns.

Add 55 g/2 oz of the butter to a saucepan, heat and stir in the flour. Cook for a few minutes without browning, remove from the heat, then add the reserved cooking liquid gradually, stirring well between each addition.

Return to the heat and gently bring to the boil, still stirring to ensure a smooth sauce. Add the cream and season to taste with salt and pepper. Pour over the fish in the dish and smooth over the surface.

To make the mash, bring a large saucepan of lightly salted water to the boil. Add the potatoes and cook for 15 –20 minutes. Drain well and mash with a potato masher until smooth. Season to taste with salt and pepper and add the remaining butter, stirring until melted.

Pile or pipe the potato onto the fish and sauce and bake in the oven for 10–15 minutes until golden brown. Serve immediately.

Vegetable Toad in the Hole

Serves 4–6

batter
100 g/3½ oz plain flour
pinch of salt
2 eggs, beaten
200 ml/7 fl oz milk
2 tbsp wholegrain mustard
2 tbsp vegetable oil

filling
25 g/1 oz butter
2 garlic cloves, crushed
1 onion, cut into eight wedges
75 g/2¾ oz baby carrots,
  halved lengthways
50 g/1¾ oz French beans
50 g/1¾ oz canned sweetcorn,
  drained
2 tomatoes, deseeded and
  cut into chunks
1 tsp wholegrain mustard
1 tbsp chopped fresh
  mixed herbs
salt and pepper

Preheat the oven to 200°C/400°F/Gas Mark 6. To make the batter, sift the flour and salt into a bowl. Beat in the eggs and milk to make a batter. Stir in the mustard and leave to stand.

Pour the oil into a shallow ovenproof dish and place in the preheated oven for 10 minutes.

To make the filling, melt the butter in a frying pan and sauté the garlic and onion, stirring constantly, for 2 minutes. Cook the carrots and beans in a saucepan of boiling water for 7 minutes, or until tender. Drain well.

Add the sweetcorn and tomatoes to the frying pan with the mustard and chopped mixed herbs. Season with salt and pepper to taste and add the carrots and beans.

Remove the preheated dish from the oven and pour in the batter over the hot oil. Spoon the vegetables into the centre, return to the oven and cook for 30–35 minutes, or until the batter has risen and set. Serve immediately.

Ploughman's Lunch

Serves 4

4 large eggs
225 g/8 oz British cheese, such as
  Cheddar, Stilton and/
  or Somerset Brie
300 g/10½ oz ready-made pork pie
1 carrot
8 spring onions
16 baby vine tomatoes
4 slices cured ham
4 tbsp chutney of your choice
85 g/3 oz salad leaves
crusty bread, to serve

Bring a saucepan of water to the boil. Gently lower the eggs into the water using a long-handled spoon. Keep the water at a gentle simmer and cook for 4–5 minutes, or until cooked to your liking. Remove the eggs and cool under cold running water.

Peel the hard-boiled eggs carefully and wipe to make sure there are no pieces of shell attached to the eggs. Cut the eggs in half. Cut the cheese into wedges and the pork pie into quarters. Peel the carrot and cut into batons. Arrange the eggs, cheese, pork pie and carrots on individual plates and add equal portions of the remaining ingredients. Serve with crusty bread.

MUDEFORD QUAY, ENGLAND

Chapter 3

Weekend Wonders

Roast Chicken

Serves 6

2.25 kg/5 lb free-range chicken
55 g/2 oz butter
2 tbsp chopped fresh lemon thyme
1 lemon, quartered
125 ml/4 fl oz white wine
salt and pepper

Preheat the oven to 220°C/425°F/Gas Mark 7.

Wipe the chicken well with kitchen paper, inside and out, and place in a roasting tin.

Place the butter in a bowl and soften with a fork, then mix in the herbs and season well with salt and pepper.

Butter the chicken all over with the herb butter, inside and out, and place the lemon pieces inside the body cavity. Pour the wine over the chicken.

Roast in the centre of the preheated oven for 20 minutes. Reduce the temperature to 190°C/375°F/Gas Mark 5 and continue to roast for a further 1¼ hours, basting frequently. If the skin is starting to brown too much, cover with foil. If the tin dries out, add a little more wine or water.

Test that the chicken is cooked by piercing the thickest part of the leg with a sharp knife or skewer and making sure the juices run clear. Remove from the oven.

Remove the chicken from the roasting tin and place on a warmed serving plate, cover with foil and leave to rest for 10 minutes before carving.

Place the roasting tin on the hob over a low heat and bubble the pan juices gently until they have reduced and are thick and glossy. Season with salt and pepper.

Serve the chicken with the pan juices.

Roast Beef

Serves 8

2.7 kg/6 lb prime rib of beef
2 tsp dry English mustard
3 tbsp plain flour
300 ml/10 fl oz red wine
300 ml/10 fl oz beef stock
2 tsp Worcestershire sauce
  (optional)
salt and pepper
Yorkshire Puddings
  (see page 72), to serve

Preheat the oven to 230°C/450°F/Gas Mark 8.

Season the meat with salt and pepper to taste and rub in the mustard and 1 tablespoon of the flour.

Place the meat in a roasting tin and cook for 15 minutes. Reduce the heat to 190°C/375°F/Gas Mark 5 and cook for 15 minutes per 450 g/1 lb, plus 15 minutes (1 hour 45 minutes for this joint) for rare beef or 20 minutes per 450 g/1 lb, plus 20 minutes (2 hours 20 minutes) for medium beef. Baste the meat from time to time to keep it moist and if the tin becomes too dry, add a little red wine or stock.

Remove the meat from the oven and place on a hot serving plate, cover with foil and leave in a warm place for 10–15 minutes.

To make the gravy, pour off most of the fat from the tin, leaving behind the meat juices and the sediment. Place the tin on the top of the hob over a medium heat and scrape all the sediment from the base of the tin. Sprinkle in the remaining flour and quickly mix it into the juices with a small whisk. When you have a smooth paste, gradually add the wine and most of the stock, whisking all the time. Bring to the boil, then turn down the heat to a gentle simmer and cook for 2–3 minutes. Season with salt and pepper to taste and add the remaining stock, if needed, and a little Worcestershire sauce, if using.

Carve the meat into slices and serve immediately with the gravy and Yorkshire Puddings.

Roast Leg of Lamb

Serves 6

1.5 kg/3 lb 5 oz leg of lamb
6 garlic cloves,
 thinly sliced lengthways
8 fresh rosemary sprigs
4 tbsp olive oil
salt and pepper

glaze
4 tbsp redcurrant jelly
300 ml/10 fl oz rosé wine

Preheat the oven to 200°C/400°F/Gas Mark 6.

Using a small knife, cut slits all over the leg of lamb. Insert 1–2 garlic slices and 4–5 rosemary needles in each slit. Place any remaining rosemary in the base of a roasting tin. Season the lamb to taste with salt and pepper and place in the roasting tin. Pour over the oil. Cover with foil and roast in the preheated oven for 1 hour 20 minutes.

To make the glaze, mix the redcurrant jelly and wine together in a small saucepan. Heat gently, stirring constantly, until combined. Bring to the boil, then reduce the heat and simmer until reduced.

Remove the lamb from the oven and pour over the glaze. Return to the oven and cook, uncovered, for about 10 minutes, depending on how well done you like the lamb.

Remove the lamb from the roasting tin, cover with foil and leave to rest for 15 minutes before carving and serving.

DORSET, ENGLAND

Beef Wellington

Serves 6

2 tbsp olive oil or vegetable oil
1.5 kg/3 lb 5 oz beef fillet, cut from
  the middle of the fillet, trimmed
  of fat and sinew
55 g/2 oz butter
150 g/5½ oz mushrooms, chopped
2 garlic cloves, crushed
150 g/5½ oz smooth liver pâté
few drops of truffle oil (optional)
1 tbsp fresh parsley, finely chopped
2 tsp English mustard
500 g/1 lb 2 oz ready-made
  puff pastry
1 egg, lightly beaten
salt and pepper
wilted greens and roasted root
  vegetables, including parsnips,
  to serve

Place a large frying pan over a high heat and add the olive oil. Rub salt and pepper into the beef, place it in the pan and sear very quickly all over. (This method gives a rare version. If you want it less rare, roast it at 200°C/400°F/Gas Mark 6, for 20 minutes at this stage.) Set aside to cool.

Heat the butter in a frying pan over a medium heat, add the mushrooms and fry for 5 minutes. Reduce the heat, add the garlic and fry for a further 5 minutes. Put the mushrooms and garlic in a bowl, add the pâté, truffle oil, if using, and parsley, and mash with a fork. Leave to cool.

Rub the mustard into the seared beef fillet. Roll out the pastry into a rectangle large enough to wrap the whole fillet with some to spare. Spread the mushroom paste in the middle of the pastry in a shape the size of the base of the beef and lay the beef on top. Brush the edges of the pastry with half of the beaten egg and fold it over, edges overlapping, and across the meat to completely enclose it.

Preheat the oven to 200°C/400°F/Gas Mark 6. Place the wrapped beef in a roasting tin with the join underneath and brush with the remaining beaten egg. Leave to chill in the refrigerator for 15 minutes, then transfer to the preheated oven and bake for 50 minutes. Check after 30 minutes – if the pastry looks golden brown, cover it with foil to prevent it burning.

Carve the beef into thick slices and serve on warmed plates with wilted greens and roasted root vegetables.

Chicken, Mushroom & Tarragon Pie

Serves 4–6

1 chicken, about 1.5 kg/3 lb 5 oz
2 fresh tarragon sprigs
1 onion, cut into wedges
300 ml/10 fl oz water
25 g/1 oz butter
175 g/6 oz chestnut mushrooms,
  sliced
2 tbsp plain flour
55 g/2 oz frozen peas or
  shelled fresh peas
1 tbsp chopped fresh tarragon
salt and pepper

pastry
225 g/8 oz plain flour,
  plus extra for dusting
pinch of salt
175 g/6 oz butter
4 tbsp iced water, plus extra
  for brushing
1 egg, beaten

Preheat the oven to 200°C/400°F/Gas Mark 6.

Put the chicken, tarragon sprigs and onion into a casserole dish, add the water and season with salt and pepper. Cover and bake in the preheated oven for 1½ hours. Remove from the oven and lift out the chicken from the casserole dish. Strain the cooking juices into a measuring jug and leave to cool.

Meanwhile, make the pastry. Sift the flour with a pinch of salt into a bowl and add the butter and water. Mix to a firm but slightly lumpy dough, adding more iced water if necessary. Roll out into a rectangle on a floured surface, then fold the top third down and the bottom third up. Give the dough a quarter turn, roll out and fold again. Repeat once more, then wrap in clingfilm and chill in the refrigerator.

Discard the chicken skin, cut off the meat and dice. Skim off the fat from the cooking juices and make up to 300 ml/10 fl oz with water.

Melt the butter in a large saucepan. Cook the mushrooms over a medium heat for 3 minutes. Stir in the flour for 1 minute, then gradually stir in the cooking juices. Bring to the boil, add the chicken, peas and tarragon and season. Transfer to a pie dish and leave to cool.

Roll out the pastry to 2.5 cm/1 inch larger than the top of the dish. Cut out a 15-mm/⅝-inch strip all the way around. Brush the rim of the dish with water and press the strip onto it. Brush with water and lift the remaining dough on top. Trim off the excess and crimp the edges to seal. Make a slit in the centre and brush with half of the egg. Roll out the trimmings and use to decorate the pie, then brush with the remaining egg. Bake in the oven for 40 minutes until golden. Serve immediately.

Shepherd's Pie

Serves 6

1 tbsp olive oil
2 onions, finely chopped
2 garlic cloves, finely chopped
675 g/1 lb 8 oz good-quality
  minced lamb
2 carrots, finely chopped
1 tbsp plain flour
225 ml/8 fl oz beef stock
  or chicken stock
125 ml/4 fl oz red wine
Worcestershire sauce (optional)
salt and pepper

mashed potato topping
675 g/1 lb 8 oz floury potatoes,
  such as King Edward, Maris Piper
  or Desirée, peeled and cut into
  chunks
55 g/2 oz butter
2 tbsp cream or milk

Preheat the oven to 180°C/350°F/Gas Mark 4.

Heat the oil in a casserole dish, add the onions and fry until soft, then add the garlic and stir well.

Increase the heat and add the meat. Cook quickly to brown the meat all over, stirring constantly. Add the carrots and season well with salt and pepper.

Stir in the flour and add the stock and wine. Stir well and heat until simmering and thickened.

Cover the casserole dish and cook in the oven for about 1 hour. Check the consistency from time to time and add a little more stock or wine if required. The meat mixture should be quite thick but not dry. Season to taste with salt and pepper and add a little Worcestershire sauce, if using.

While the meat is cooking, make the mashed potato topping. Bring a large saucepan of lightly salted water to the boil, add the potatoes and cook for 15–20 minutes. Drain well and mash with a potato masher until smooth. Add the butter and cream and season well with salt and pepper.

Spoon the lamb mixture into an ovenproof serving dish and spread or pipe the potato on top.

Increase the oven temperature to 200°C/400°F/Gas Mark 6 and cook the pie for 15–20 minutes at the top of the oven until golden brown. You might like to finish it off under a medium grill for a really crisp brown topping to the potato. Serve immediately.

Poached Salmon with Hollandaise Sauce

Serves 8

melted butter, for greasing
1.8 kg/4 lb whole fresh salmon,
  gutted
1 lemon, sliced
sprigs of fresh flat-leaf parsley,
  plus extra to garnish
125 ml/4 fl oz white wine or water
salt and pepper
lemon wedges, to serve

hollandaise sauce
2 tbsp white wine vinegar
2 tbsp water
6 black peppercorns
3 egg yolks
250 g/9 oz unsalted butter
2 tsp lemon juice

Preheat the oven to 150°C/300°F/Gas Mark 2. Line a roasting tin with a double layer of foil and brush with butter.

Trim off the fins then season the salmon with salt and pepper, inside and out. Lay on the foil and place the lemon slices and parsley in the body cavity. Pour over the wine and gather up the foil to make a fairly loose parcel.

Place the tin in the preheated oven and bake for 50–60 minutes. Test the salmon with the point of a knife: the flesh should flake when the fish is cooked. Remove from the oven and leave to stand for 15 minutes before removing from the foil to serve hot. To serve cold, leave for 1–2 hours until lukewarm, then carefully remove from the foil and peel away the skin from the top side, leaving the head and tail intact.

Meanwhile, to make the hollandaise sauce, put the vinegar and water into a small saucepan with the peppercorns, bring to the boil, then reduce the heat and simmer until it is reduced to 1 tablespoon (take care: this happens very quickly), then strain.

Mix the egg yolks in a blender or food processor and add the strained vinegar while the machine is running.

Melt the butter in a small saucepan and heat until it almost turns brown. Again, while the blender is running, add three quarters of the butter, the lemon juice and the remaining butter and season well with salt and pepper.

Turn the sauce into a serving bowl or keep warm for up to 1 hour in a bowl over a saucepan of warm water. To serve cold, leave to cool and store in the refrigerator for up to 2 days.

Garnish the salmon with parsley and serve with lemon wedges and hollandaise sauce on the side.

Mixed Nut Roast with Cranberry & Red Wine Sauce

Serves 4

2 tbsp butter, plus extra for
  greasing
2 garlic cloves, chopped
1 large onion, chopped
50 g/1¾ oz pine kernels, toasted
75 g/2¾ oz hazelnuts, toasted
50 g/1¾ oz walnuts, ground
50 g/1¾ oz cashew nuts, ground
100 g/3½ oz wholemeal
  breadcrumbs
1 egg, lightly beaten
2 tbsp chopped fresh thyme
250 ml/9 fl oz vegetable stock
salt and pepper
sprigs of fresh thyme, to garnish

cranberry & red wine sauce
175 g/6 oz fresh cranberries
100 g/3½ oz caster sugar
300 ml/10 fl oz red wine
1 cinnamon stick

Preheat the oven to 180°C/350°F/Gas Mark 4. Grease a loaf tin and line with greaseproof paper.

Melt the butter in a saucepan over a medium heat. Add the garlic and onion and cook, stirring, for about 3 minutes.

Remove the pan from the heat. Grind the pine kernels, hazelnuts, walnuts and cashews and stir into the pan. Add the breadcrumbs, egg, thyme, stock and seasoning.

Spoon the mixture into the loaf tin and level the surface. Cook in the centre of the preheated oven for 30 minutes or until cooked through and golden. The loaf is cooked when a skewer inserted into the centre comes out clean.

Halfway through the cooking time, make the sauce. Put all the ingredients in a saucepan and bring to the boil. Reduce the heat and simmer, stirring occasionally, for 15 minutes.

Remove the nut roast from the oven and turn out. Garnish with sprigs of thyme and serve with the sauce.

EDINBURGH CASTLE, SCOTLAND

Yorkshire Puddings

Serves 4

100 g/3½ oz plain flour
pinch of salt
1 egg, beaten
300 ml/10 fl oz milk and water
   mixed (half milk, half water)
3 tbsp roast beef dripping,
   goose fat or olive oil
pepper

Preheat the oven to 220°C/425°F/Gas Mark 7.

Place the flour and a pinch of salt in a mixing bowl. Make a well in the centre, then add the egg and half the liquid. Using a whisk, beat the egg and milk and water mixture together and gradually incorporate the flour. Continue beating until the mixture is smooth and there are no lumps. Gradually beat in the remaining liquid. Season to taste with pepper.

Put a little dripping into each mould of a 12-hole bun tin. Heat at the top of the preheated oven for 3–4 minutes until very hot. Remove the hot tray very carefully, use a ladle to pour some batter into each mould, then return the tray to the oven.

Bake for 20–25 minutes until the Yorkshire puddings are well puffed up and golden brown. Serve immediately.

GOLD HILL, ENGLAND

Perfect Roast Potatoes

Serves 6

1.3 kg/3 lb large floury potatoes, such as King Edward, Maris Piper or Desirée, peeled and cut into even-sized chunks
3 tbsp dripping, goose fat, duck fat or olive oil
salt

Preheat the oven to 220°C/425°F/Gas Mark 7.

Bring a large saucepan of lightly salted water to the boil, add the potatoes and cook over a medium heat, covered, for 5–7 minutes. They will still be firm. Remove from the heat.

Meanwhile, add the fat to a roasting tin and place in the preheated oven.

Drain the potatoes well and return them to the pan. Cover with the lid and firmly shake the pan so that the surface of the potatoes is roughened. This will help give a much crisper texture.

Remove the tin from the oven and carefully tip the potatoes into the hot oil. Baste them to ensure they are all coated with the oil.

Roast at the top of the oven for 45–50 minutes until they are browned all over and thoroughly crisp. Turn the potatoes and baste again only once during the process or the crunchy edges will be destroyed.

Carefully transfer the potatoes from the tin into a warmed serving dish. Sprinkle with a little salt and serve immediately.

Chapter 4

To Finish

Rhubarb Crumble

Serves 6

900 g/2 lb rhubarb
115 g/4 oz caster sugar
grated rind and juice of
 1 orange
cream, yogurt or custard,
 to serve

crumble topping
225 g/8 oz plain flour or
 wholemeal flour
115 g/4 oz unsalted butter
115 g/4 oz soft light
 brown sugar
1 tsp ground ginger

Preheat the oven to 190°C/375°F/Gas Mark 5.

Cut the rhubarb into 2.5-cm/1-inch lengths and place in a 1.7-litre/3-pint ovenproof dish with the sugar and the orange rind and juice.

Make the crumble topping by placing the flour in a mixing bowl and rubbing in the butter until the mixture resembles breadcrumbs. Stir in the sugar and the ginger.

Spread the crumble evenly over the fruit and press down lightly using a fork. Bake in the centre of the preheated oven on a baking tray for 25–30 minutes until the crumble is golden brown. Serve with cream.

SOUTH COAST, ENGLAND

Wensleydale Apple Pie

Serves 6–8

350 g/12 oz plain flour
pinch of salt
100 g/3½ oz butter, plus extra
  for greasing
100 g/3½ oz Wensleydale
  cheese, grated
2 egg yolks
3 tbsp water
900 g/2 lb cooking apples, peeled,
  cored and thinly sliced
115 g/4 oz caster sugar
½ tsp ground cinnamon
½ tsp ground cloves
1 egg white
175 g/6 oz Wensleydale cheese,
  sliced, to serve

Grease a 23-cm/9-inch tart tin.

Sift the flour and salt into a mixing bowl and gently rub in the butter until the mixture resembles breadcrumbs. Add the grated cheese and rub in. Add the egg yolks and mix together with the water to form a soft dough.

Knead lightly until the pastry is smooth. Cover with clingfilm and chill in the refrigerator for 30 minutes.

Preheat the oven to 200°C/400°F/Gas Mark 6.

Roll out two-thirds of the pastry and use to line the tin.

Layer in the sliced apples with all but 1 teaspoon of the sugar and the spices.

Roll out the remaining pastry, dampen the edges of the pastry lining the tin with water and lay the rolled pastry on top. Press down well to seal the edges and cut away any excess pastry. Crimp the edges with a fork.

Beat the egg white and use to glaze the pie, sprinkling the remaining sugar over to give a crisp finish.

Bake in the preheated oven for 40–45 minutes, or until the pastry is crisp and golden.

Cut the pie into portions. Slip a slice of cheese under the crust of each piece and serve immediately.

Bread & Butter Pudding

Serves 4–6

85 g/3 oz butter, softened
6 slices thick white bread
55 g/2 oz mixed fruit
   (sultanas, currants and raisins)
25 g/1 oz candied peel
3 large eggs
300 ml/10 fl oz milk
150 ml/5 fl oz double cream
55 g/2 oz caster sugar
whole nutmeg, for grating
1 tbsp demerara sugar
cream, to serve

Preheat the oven to 180°C/350°F/Gas Mark 4.

Use a little of the butter to grease a 20 x 25-cm/8 x 10-inch baking dish and the remainder to butter the slices of bread. Cut the bread slices into quarters and arrange half overlapping in the dish.

Scatter half the dried fruit and candied peel over the bread, cover with the remaining bread slices and add the remaining fruit and peel.

In a mixing jug, whisk the eggs well and mix in the milk, cream and sugar. Pour this over the pudding and leave to stand for 15 minutes to allow the bread to soak up some of the egg mixture. Tuck in most of the fruit as you do not want it to burn in the oven. Grate the nutmeg over the top of the pudding, according to taste, and sprinkle over the demerara sugar.

Place the pudding on a baking tray and bake at the top of the preheated oven for 30–40 minutes until just set and golden brown.

Remove from the oven and serve warm with cream.

Treacle Tart

Serves 8

250 g/ 9 oz ready-made
  shortcrust pastry
plain flour, for dusting
350 g/12 oz golden syrup
125 g/4½ oz fresh white
  breadcrumbs
125 ml/4 fl oz double cream
finely grated rind of ½ lemon
  or orange
2 tbsp lemon juice or orange juice
whipped cream or clotted cream,
  to serve

Roll out the pastry on a lightly floured work surface and use to line a 20-cm/8-inch round loose-based tart tin, reserving the pastry trimmings. Prick the base of the pastry case all over with a fork, cover with clingfilm and chill in the refrigerator for 30 minutes. Re-roll the reserved pastry trimmings and cut out small shapes, such as hearts, leaves or stars, to decorate the top of the tart.

Preheat the oven to 190°C/375°F/Gas Mark 5.

Mix the golden syrup, breadcrumbs, double cream and lemon rind with the lemon juice in a small bowl. Pour the mixture into the pastry case and decorate the top of the tart with the pastry shapes.

Transfer to the preheated oven and bake for 35–40 minutes, or until the filling is just set.

Leave the tart to cool slightly in the tin, then turn out and serve with cream.

BRECON BEACONS, WALES

Sticky Toffee Pudding

Serves 6–8

pudding
75 g/2¾ oz sultanas
150 g/5½ oz stoned dates, chopped
1 tsp bicarbonate of soda
25 g/1 oz butter, plus extra
  for greasing
200 g/7 oz soft light
  brown sugar
2 eggs
200 g/7 oz self-raising flour, sifted

sticky toffee sauce
25 g/1 oz butter
175 ml/6 fl oz double cream
200 g/7 oz soft light brown sugar

Preheat the oven to 180°C/350°F/Gas Mark 4. Grease a 20-cm/8-inch round cake tin.

To make the pudding, put the sultanas, dates and bicarbonate of soda into a heatproof bowl. Cover with boiling water and leave to soak. Put the butter into a separate bowl, add the sugar and mix well. Beat in the eggs, then fold in the flour. Drain the soaked fruit, add to the bowl and mix.

Spoon the mixture evenly into the prepared cake tin. Bake in the preheated oven for 35–40 minutes, or until a skewer inserted into the centre comes out clean.

About 5 minutes before the end of the cooking time, make the sauce. Melt the butter in a saucepan over a medium heat. Stir in the cream and sugar and bring to the boil, stirring constantly. Reduce the heat and simmer for 5 minutes.

Cut the pudding into equal-sized portions, pour over the sauce and serve immediately.

GIANT'S CAUSEWAY, NORTHERN IRELAND

Spotted Dick & Custard

Serves 6

225 g/8 oz self-raising flour
115 g/4 oz suet
55 g/2 oz caster sugar
140 g/5 oz currants or raisins
grated rind of 1 lemon
150–175 ml/5–6 fl oz milk
2 tsp melted butter, for greasing

custard
425 ml/15 fl oz single cream
5 egg yolks
3 tbsp caster sugar
½ tsp vanilla extract
1 tsp cornflour (optional)

Put the flour, suet, sugar, currants and lemon rind into a mixing bowl and mix together well.

Pour in the milk and stir to give a fairly soft dough.

Turn out the dough onto a floured surface and roll into a cylinder. Wrap in greaseproof paper that has been well-buttered and seal the ends, leaving room for the pudding to rise. Over-wrap with foil and place in a steamer over a saucepan of boiling water.

Steam for about 1–1½ hours, checking the water level in the saucepan from time to time.

To make the custard, heat the cream in a small saucepan just to boiling point. Cream the egg yolks, sugar and vanilla extract together in a measuring jug. You can add the cornflour to this cold egg yolk mixture to ensure the sauce does not separate. Pour the hot cream into the jug, stirring all the time. Return the mixture to the saucepan.

Heat the custard very gently, stirring constantly, until the sauce has just thickened, then remove from the heat. Alternatively, you can cook the custard in a bowl over a saucepan of simmering water to prevent overcooking.

Remove the pudding from the steamer and unwrap. Place on a warmed plate and cut into thick slices. Serve with the custard.

Eton Mess

Serves 4–6

3 egg whites
175 g/6 oz caster sugar
700 g/1 lb 9 oz strawberries, hulled
2 tbsp icing sugar
2 tbsp crème de fraise (optional)
300 ml/10 fl oz double cream
150 ml/5 fl oz single cream

Preheat the oven to 150°C/300°F/Gas Mark 2.

Whisk the egg whites in a mixing bowl using an electric mixer until thick and in soft peaks. Add the sugar gradually, whisking well after each addition. The meringue mixture should be glossy and firm.

Spoon the meringue onto a baking tray lined with baking paper and spread into a rough 30-cm/12-inch round. Cook in the preheated oven for 45–50 minutes until the meringue is firm on the outside but still soft in the centre. Remove from the oven and allow to cool.

Place a third of the strawberries (choose the larger ones) in a food processor or blender and purée with the icing sugar. Pour the purée into a bowl, add the liqueur, if using, and the remaining strawberries and turn in the sauce until well mixed.

Whip together the double and single cream until thick but still light and floppy.

Break the meringue into large pieces and place half in a large glass serving bowl. Spoon over half the fruit mixture and half the cream. Layer up the remaining ingredients and lightly fold the mixtures together so you have a streaky appearance.

Serve immediately after mixing or the meringues will soften.

 # Cornish Ice Cream

Serves 4

400 ml/14 fl oz double cream
150 ml/5 fl oz whole milk
  (or Cornish milk, if available)
4 egg yolks
85 g/3 oz caster sugar
115 g/4 oz Cornish clotted cream
½ tsp vanilla extract (optional)

Pour the cream and milk into a heavy-based saucepan and place over a low heat. Slowly bring to a simmer and remove from the heat.

Beat the egg yolks with the sugar in a mixing bowl with a hand mixer until thick and pale.

Pour the hot cream mixture onto the yolks and whisk thoroughly.

Return the mixture to the rinsed-out saucepan and heat very gently until the sauce has just thickened. It should just coat the back of a wooden spoon. Immediately place the base of the saucepan in a bowl of cold water to prevent it overcooking. Pour into a cool bowl and when almost cold, whisk in the clotted cream and vanilla extract, if using.

Transfer to an ice-cream machine and churn according to the instructions. Alternatively, freeze the mixture in a rigid freezerproof box for 1 hour. Remove from the freezer and break up the ice cream with a fork to break down the ice crystals. Beat well and return to the freezer for a further hour and repeat the process until the mixture is completely frozen.

Remove the ice cream from the freezer and place in the refrigerator for 15–30 minutes before serving.

Home-made Oat Crackers with British Cheeses

Makes about 30 crackers

115 g/4 oz wholemeal flour,
  plus extra for rolling
1 tsp baking powder
½ tsp salt
140 g/5 oz fine oatmeal
85 g/3 oz butter,
  plus extra for greasing
1 tbsp caster sugar
4 tbsp cold water

to serve
British cheeses, such as Cheddar,
  Somerset Brie, Stilton and
  Cornish Yarg
grapes and figs

Preheat the oven to 180°C/350°F/Gas Mark 4 and lightly grease 2 baking sheets.

Sieve the flour, baking powder and salt into a mixing bowl, then mix in the oatmeal. Add the butter and rub it into the dry ingredients. Spoon in the sugar and the water and mix to a smooth dough. Turn the mixture onto a floured surface and knead until smooth.

Roll the dough out until 3 mm/⅛ inch thick, then cut out the crackers using a 6-cm/2½-inch round cutter.

Place the biscuits onto the prepared baking sheets and bake for about 15 minutes until golden. Change the position of the sheets in the oven halfway through the cooking time to ensure even cooking. Remove from the oven and lift the biscuits onto a wire rack to cool.

Serve the oat crackers with a variety of British cheeses.

apples
  Pork & Apple Pie 15
  Wensleydale Apple Pie 80
apricots: Coronation Chicken 46

beef
  Beef Stew with Dumplings 43
  Beef Wellington 62
  Cornish Pasties 27
  Mustard Steak Sandwiches 18
  Roast Beef 58
  Roast Beef & Horseradish
    Sandwiches 16
  Steak & Kidney Pudding 34
bread
  Bread & Butter Pudding 83
  Ploughman's Lunch 52
  Treacle Tart 84
  Welsh Rarebit 22
  see also sandwiches
Broccoli & Stilton Soup 10
Bubble & Squeak 24

cabbage: Bubble & Squeak 24
carrots
  Coronation Chicken 46
  Irish Stew 44
  Shepherd's Pie 67
  Vegetable Toad in the Hole 50
cheese
  Broccoli & Stilton Soup 10
  Home-made Oat Crackers with
    British Cheeses 95
  Ploughman's Lunch 52
  Smoked Salmon & Cream Cheese
    Sandwiches 16
  Welsh Rarebit 22
  Wensleydale Apple Pie 80
chicken
  Chicken, Mushroom & Tarragon
    Pie 64
  Coronation Chicken 46
  Roast Chicken 56
Cornish Ice Cream 92
Cornish Pasties 27
Coronation Chicken 46
cranberries: Mixed Nut Roast with
  Cranberry & Red Wine Sauce 70
Cucumber Sandwiches 16

dates: Sticky Toffee Pudding 86
dried fruit
  Bread & Butter Pudding 83
  Spotted Dick & Custard 89
  Sticky Toffee Pudding 86

eggs
  Egg & Cress Sandwiches 16
  Gammon Steaks with Fried Egg &
    Chips 38
  Ploughman's Lunch 52
  Quiche Lorraine 12
  Scotch Eggs 28

Eton Mess 90

fish
  Fish & Chips 32
  Fish Cakes 21
  Fisherman's Pie 49
  Poached Salmon with Hollandaise
    Sauce 68
  Smoked Salmon & Cream Cheese
    Sandwiches 16
  French beans: Vegetable Toad in the
    Hole 50

Gammon Steaks with Fried Egg &
  Chips 38

ham
  Gammon Steaks with Fried Egg &
    Chips 38
  Ploughman's Lunch 52

Irish Stew 44

lamb
  Irish Stew 44
  Lancashire Hotpot 37
  Roast Leg of Lamb 61
  Shepherd's Pie 67
Lancashire Hotpot 37
lemons
  Spotted Dick & Custard 89
  Treacle Tart 84

mushrooms
  Beef Wellington 62
  Chicken, Mushroom & Tarragon
    Pie 64
  Fisherman's Pie 49
  Steak & Kidney Pudding 34
Mustard Steak Sandwiches 18

nuts: Mixed Nut Roast with Cranberry
  & Red Wine Sauce 70

oranges
  Rhubarb Crumble 78
  Treacle Tart 84

peas: Chicken, Mushroom & Tarragon
  Pie 64
pies & tarts
  Beef Wellington 62
  Chicken, Mushroom & Tarragon
    Pie 64
  Cornish Pasties 27
  Pork & Apple Pie 15
  Treacle Tart 84
  Wensleydale Apple Pie 80
Ploughman's Lunch 52
Pork & Apple Pie 15
potatoes
  Broccoli & Stilton Soup 10
  Bubble & Squeak 24

Cornish Pasties 27
Fish & Chips 32
Fish Cakes 21
Fisherman's Pie 49
Gammon Steaks with Fried Egg &
  Chips 38
Irish Stew 44
Lancashire Hotpot 37
Perfect Roast Potatoes 74
Pork & Apple Pie 15
Sausage & Mash with Onion
  Gravy 40
Shepherd's Pie 67
prawns: Fisherman's Pie 49
puddings
  Bread & Butter Pudding 83
  Cornish Ice Cream 92
  Eton Mess 90
  Rhubarb Crumble 78
  Spotted Dick & Custard 89
  Sticky Toffee Pudding 86
  Treacle Tart 84
  Wensleydale Apple Pie 80

Quiche Lorraine 12

Rhubarb Crumble 78
Roast Beef 58
Roast Chicken 56
Roast Leg of Lamb 61

salmon
  Poached Salmon with Hollandaise
    Sauce 68
  Smoked Salmon & Cream Cheese
    Sandwiches 16
sandwiches
  Classic Sandwich Selection 16
  Mustard Steak Sandwiches 18
sausages
  Sausage & Mash with Onion
    Gravy 40
  Scotch Eggs 28
Scotch Eggs 28
Shepherd's Pie 67
soup: Broccoli & Stilton Soup 10
Spotted Dick & Custard 89
Steak & Kidney Pudding 34
Sticky Toffee Pudding 86
strawberries: Eton Mess 90
swede: Cornish Pasties 27
sweetcorn: Vegetable Toad in the
  Hole 50

tomatoes
  Ploughman's Lunch 52
  Vegetable Toad in the Hole 50
Treacle Tart 84

Vegetable Toad in the Hole 50

Welsh Rarebit 22
Wensleydale Apple Pie 80